Here are

101

tips for you to grow up happy and successful.

To get the best out of life,

AIM
HIGH!

SECOND EDITION
www.aimhigh101tips.com

Inquiries Contact:
bradberger29@gmail.com

Book designed by Larry Rubenstein

ISBN: 978-0-615-33022-8
Published by AIM HIGH! 101 TIPS, LLC

This book is for you.
It is for teenagers
everywhere.

The 101 Tips in this book
will make you a happier
person and a better person.

You already know many
of the tips and they are
already part of your life.

AIM HIGH! is your guide
for school and for life.

TABLE OF CONTENTS

Think!

Think before
you do something.

Consider the
alternatives before
you act.

Careful thinking
produces the best
results.

**Ethics and morals
are important.**

Ethics are the moral
standards and rules
of correct conduct.

An ethical person
has the ability to pick
and choose the
proper way to act.

Take pride in
acting correctly.

**Have a positive
attitude.**

Be a positive person.

You can think only one
thought at a time –
make it a positive one.

Look for the good in
every experience,
situation, and person.

Develop your goals.

Goals are what you want to achieve.

Make a plan and imagine yourself achieving your goals.

Your imagination and your work each day will help you achieve your goals.

4

Persistence pays.

Persistent people
accomplish what they set
out to do.

They act consistently
until they reach a goal.

Persistent people
achieve their goals.

5

Make commitments, keep your word.

Follow through on the commitments you make.

Keeping commitments earns respect and trust from others.

You will become a stronger and better person if you keep your word.

Tell the truth.

Telling the truth is the right way to act.

Living with lies is harder than living a truthful life.

Being truthful and honest is important.

Make a good impression.

Always make a good impression.

Put your best foot forward.

First impressions are very important.

Neatness counts.

It is easier to function in a neat and orderly space than a mess.

You will feel better when your appearance and your environment are neat.

Good health.

Develop habits that keep you healthy.

Maintaining good health is your decision and a lifelong choice.

You can make yourself healthy.

Good health is the most important thing you have.

10

**Keep your hands
clean; wash them as
often as possible.**

Clean hands help to keep
you healthy.

Wash your hands with
soap and water for
at least 15 seconds.

Keep your hands clean.
Keep yourself healthy.

**Eat fruits and
vegetables, they are
good for you.**

Eat fruits and
vegetables every day.

They will energize you,
control your weight,
and keep you healthy.

Seven is the lucky
number of fruits and
veggies to eat each day.

Eat a good breakfast.

Start your day in
a healthy way.

Eat nutritious foods
that give you the energy
your body needs to
maintain your maximum
efficiency throughout
the day.

Breakfast keeps
you awake.

Don't smoke!

Never smoke.

Smoking causes cancer. It also causes heart and lung disease and other fatal diseases.

If you have started smoking, quit now.

If you can't quit, get help. You can do it!

Smoking can kill you.

Avoid drugs!

If you use drugs you hurt your mind and your body and you are breaking the law.

Maintain your health and happiness by saying NO and not using drugs.

If you have a drug habit, seek help from family, friends and professionals.

Drive soberly.

To drink, or to do
drugs and to drive is
a way to death.

Take a taxi, public
transportation, or stay
where you are.

Your parent, an adult or
a friend will be much
happier to pick you up
anywhere when you are
intoxicated rather than
seeing you injured.

Never ride in a car with
a driver who is drinking
or taking drugs!

16

Exercise.

Exercise is important for your physical and mental well-being.

Develop an exercise routine and you acquire a healthy habit for life.

Enjoy your exercise.

Relax.

Take a break.

Sit by yourself in a
calm and quiet place.

Close your eyes.
Breathe deeply for
a few minutes.

Read a book, watch a
television program or
listen to music.

Find a method of
relaxation that works
for you.

18

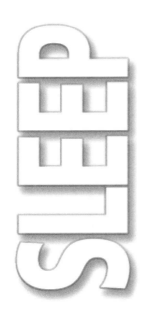

Get enough sleep.

Teenagers need more sleep than adults.

Doctors recommend that teens get between 10 and 12 hours of sleep each night.

Teenagers physically need extra sleep.

Be modest.

Avoid bragging.

Be a humble person.

Respect people.

Respect people in
the same way that you
want to be respected.

Respecting others is
the best way to earn
respect for yourself.

**Be supportive of
your family.**

Spend time with
your family and learn
from them.

Get to know and enjoy
your relatives.

22

**Listen to the
person responsible
for your care.**

Think about what a
parent or caring
adult says to you.

If you disagree, disagree
in a respectful manner.

A caring adult usually
has your best interest
in mind when making a
decision affecting
your life.

Talk to a relative.

If you have a problem, try talking to a person who loves you and wants the best for you.

A relative is often a good choice.

24

If you are going to be out late, call to let someone know.

Do not go out or stay out late without letting someone know where you are.

It is wise to be cautious.

People must be informed of where you are to protect your safety.

25

**If your parents fight
or separate, remember
you are not at fault.**

If parents fight,
separate, or divorce,
it is not your fault.

If you are upset, speak
to a friend or a relative
and consider seeking
help from your school's
guidance counselor
or psychologist.

Be loyal.

Stay loyal to the people you like.

Stand by their side when they need you.

Your loyalty will be appreciated.

Be a good friend.

To have a good
friend you need to
be a good friend.

Do things for and
with your friend
that you might not
do with anybody else.

Good friends are special
people.

28

Respect the opposite sex.

There are many differences and similarities between girls and boys, men and women.

Respect the similarities and differences.

29

Accept responsibility.

Take responsibility
for what you do.

Be a good person.

Learn in school.

Pay attention in class, respect your teachers, and learn.

Learn as much as you can.

Do your homework.

Take your time and concentrate on your homework.

If you need help, ask your friends and family.

Complete your homework on time and do your best work.

Reading is necessary.

Read something
you truly enjoy.

It could be the sports
section of a newspaper,
a magazine, or a book.

The more you read,
the easier it is to read.

**Develop a good
vocabulary.**

When you find
a word you don't
know, look it up in a
dictionary, write down
the definition and use
the word.

As you learn more
words, you will be able
to express yourself
better when either
speaking or writing.

Learn another language.

Learn a foreign language.

If you are lucky to live with others who speak another language, you might want to learn their language.

Learning another language will help you throughout your life.

Use a computer.

A computer will give you the power to do everything from playing games to communicating with people throughout the world.

When you are on the Internet beware of people you do not know and do not give them personal information.

Use a computer to enrich your life.

**Go to movies and
watch television.**

It's fun to go to movies
and watch television.

Be selective. See movies
and programs that relax
you, entertain you, and
educate you.

Listen to music.

The sound of music is one of life's pleasures.

Whether it is rap, disco, hip-hop, jazz, or opera, music is beautiful.

Listen and make your own choices.

38

Get a hobby.

Your hobby is a special interest you really enjoy.

You can listen to music, collect things, paint, write, or participate in sports.

Have fun with your hobby.

**Be creative and enjoy
your creativity.**

Artists, athletes,
corporate presidents,
and children are
creative.

You can be creative
in school, at home, or
with your friends.

You can be creative in
sports, in art, in music,
with words, or with a
computer.

Allow yourself
to be creative.

Perfection.

People are not perfect.

Be happy being
yourself.

Be a nice person.

A nice person is pleasant to others.

Be a kind, understanding and charitable person.

People who are nice have a good attitude.

Being nice is nice.

42

Empathize with others.

Empathy is your ability to identify with another person and understand their feelings and situation.

Empathy allows you to form an understanding with someone else.

When you can empathize with another person you are in touch with their feelings.

Be fair.

What seems fair to one person may not seem fair to another.

When you are fair with people, it is more likely that they will treat you fairly.

Show appreciation.

Everyone wants to
be appreciated.

Express appreciation
to others.

Courtesy counts.

Hold the door for somebody. Don't push when you are standing in line. Give up your seat to an elderly person on a bus or train.

When you are courteous, people will be courteous to you.

"Please" and "thank you" are really magic words.

By saying "please" and "thank you," people show themselves to be thoughtful, respectful, and nice.

Use the best table manners.

People judge you by your manners.

Learn proper table manners.

Practice your manners, and they will become good habits.

48

Avoid rude words.

Avoid rude or crude words that might hurt or embarrass other people.

Always consider what affect your words will have.

**Communicate
constructively.**

Get to the point.

Communicate clearly
when you speak, write
or e-mail.

Speak clearly and maintain eye contact.

Don't mumble.

Look directly at the other person, maintain eye contact, and speak clearly.

When you have something to say, say it.

Speak up and then listen.

It is important to express your opinions.

There are situations that require listening.

Once you have made your point, stop talking and listen.

Ask questions.

Asking questions
does not show a lack
of knowledge, but
rather the search for
knowledge.

Ask questions in a
thoughtful and polite
manner.

Learn from the
answers.

Hear advice.

When a person gives you advice, listen.

You may accept or reject the advice.

The decision is yours.

Help others.

If you know someone
needs help, help.

Join a team.

Join a team such as a sports team, a club, or a volunteer organization.

Teams teach individuals to work and play with others.

Plan to win and you will be a winner.

Tell yourself several times each day that you are a winner and you will accomplish what you want.

A winning attitude creates a winner.

**Winning isn't always
everything.**

No person or team
wins all the time.

Don't dwell on losses.

Look forward to the next
time you will win.

Keep your confidence
and your next win
will be sooner than
you think.

Everyone makes mistakes.

We all make mistakes.

Learn to avoid making the same mistakes twice.

Seek help.

Don't be embarrassed
to ask for help.

People like to help
each other.

Seek help from the best
person available.

Show your appreciation
to the person helping
you.

60

Sorry.

If you hurt someone's feelings, apologize.

If you make a mistake, apologize.

Saying "I'm sorry" will make you and the other person feel better.

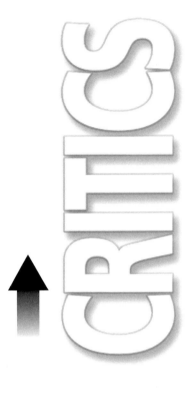

Learn to deal with criticism.

No one likes to be criticized.

Deal with the criticism in a positive way.

Don't blame the messenger. Just listen to the message and do your best.

Forgive.

Show forgiveness
in your heart and in
your mind.

Be a forgiving person.

63

**Violence is not
the solution.**

Talk out your problems,
don't fight about them.

Listen, speak, and
resolve your differences.

Be a peaceful person.

Plan your life.

Don't leave your life to chance.

Think about what you want to achieve.

Learn a skill, follow your passion or plan something else.

Your life belongs to you.

Follow the rules.

Know the rules
and go with them.

Breaking rules causes
punishment and other
bad consequences.

Follow rules.

Use time wisely.

Plan your activities
so that you can
accomplish all you
want.

Keep motivated.

Motivation is the desire to achieve and accomplish what you want in life.

Keep yourself motivated and enjoy your progress.

**Take one step
at a time.**

Every goal has
many steps.

Go step by step.

Accomplish something
each day and you will
accomplish what you
want in life.

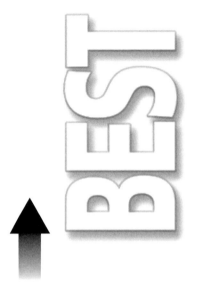

**Try hard –
do your best.**

Always strive to
do your best.

Your extra efforts,
giving 100 percent,
giving it your all will
lead to the extraordinary
accomplishments in
your life.

If you try hard and
keep a positive
attitude, you will
always do your best.

Reward yourself.

When you achieve something, reward yourself.

Buy yourself a present, go to a movie, do a special fun activity.

You deserve to reward yourself when you achieve things in your life.

Practice, practice, practice...

To be good at anything you need to practice.

No one is a champion or a gold-medal winner without practice.

People born with extraordinary talents still must practice their skills.

Practice with a positive attitude and you will succeed.

Try, try, try again.

Work your way around obstacles.

Don't give up until you have tried all of the proper ways to achieve your goal.

Keep trying and you will succeed.

Some days are better than others.

Everyone has good and bad days.

Life is not one steady flow of good or bad events.

Try to remember the good in each day.

When things are bad, keep your positive spirit and remember tomorrow will be a better day.

Be careful.

Be careful about the way you lead your life.

Think and use good judgment in what you say and do.

**Stand up for
yourself.**

Don't let bullies push
you around.

Stand up for what you
believe in, and, if you
feel threatened, do not
hesitate to speak to a
teacher or a parent or
other adult.

76

Be flexible.

Flexibility allows you to adjust to change in a constructive way.

Change can be difficult but necessary.

Be flexible.

Life is full of compromises.

No one gets their way all the time.

Learn to compromise and you will get what you want most of the time.

**Don't feel sorry
for yourself.**

Bad things happen
to everyone.

Don't get stuck in
self-pity.

Focus your energies
on being positive and
regaining your spirit.

SPIRIT

Express anger in a constructive way.

Learn to deal with anger in a constructive way and non-violent way.

Some people scream, some people rip things up, and some people keep the anger inside of them.

If you are angry at someone, let them know your feelings.

When you let go of your anger, you will feel better.

It's okay to cry.

Crying is an important expression of human emotion.

Don't be embarrassed to cry.

Presidents, athletes, and just regular people cry.

A good cry can make you feel better.

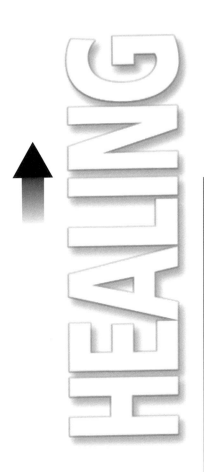

Time heals.

Some wounds take longer to heal than others.

As time passes your hurts, your injuries, and your mind and body will heal.

Have a Win/Win attitude.

Any situation is better if both people can be winners.

If you can convince another person that your position is correct and, at the same time, the other person gains something, then you have created a Win/Win situation.

People fail.

Failure is part of life.

Because you fail does
not make you a failure.

Learn from the failure.

Put it behind you
and move on.

Believe in yourself.

When you believe in
yourself, you have the
ability to do almost
anything you set your
mind, heart, and body to.

Have confidence in your
ability to succeed, and
you will.

85

Be enthusiastic.

Enthusiasm is the joy you show when doing your daily activities.

When you are enthusiastic, whatever you are doing becomes more pleasurable.

Enthusiasm is contagious.

86

View problems as challenges.

Problems are challenges to overcome.

Face problems and handle them quickly.

Use your creativity, imagination, common sense, and intuition to solve problems.

87

Think happy.

Think happy thoughts.

When you are down,
replace your negative
thoughts with positive,
happy thoughts.

Let your thoughts
be happy throughout
your day.

88

Smile.

When you smile,
people around you
smile with you.

A smile cheers up a
room, makes a difficult
situation more pleasant,
and creates good
feelings among people.

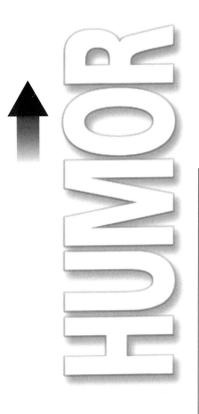

**Develop a sense
of humor.**

A sense of humor
makes both the serious
moments in life and
the lighter moments
more enjoyable.

It is good to laugh
at yourself as well
as to enjoy another
person's humor.

Lighten up!

Play.

Find an activity that you enjoy and have fun doing it.

Enjoy nature.

Trees, the sky, the birds, and weather are true wonders of nature.

Take time to enjoy the natural wonders that are a part of your world.

Preserve the environment.

Have heroes.

Heroes are women and men of excellence who did great things.

Model yourself after your heroes.

93

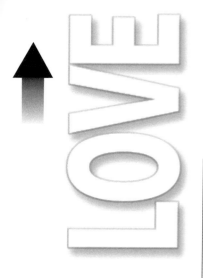

You are loved.

You are loved by
many people.

People show love in
different ways.

Learn to recognize
different types of love.

Show love to those
you love.

Dream.

Dream the possible
and the impossible.

If you dream something
often enough, it becomes
a goal in your life.

Dreams come true when
you achieve your goals.

Miracles happen.

Things happen in life that can't be explained.

Miracles do happen.

Begin again.

Starting something is the first step to completion.

Don't be afraid to start again.

If you don't begin, you can't reach the end.

**Be proud; take pride in
yourself.**

Keep your positive
mental attitude and, try
your best, and you
will feel proud about
yourself.

Be courageous.

Courage conquers fear.

Be courageous!

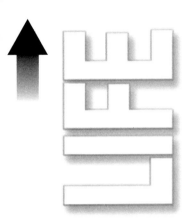

Love life.

Life is good.

Enjoy yourself
and be happy.

100

AIM HIGH!

Enjoy your life.

MY THOUGHTS...

Think!

Think!

Think!

Think!

Think!

Think!

Think!

Think!

Think!

Think!

Think!

Think!

Think!

Think!

Think!

Think!

Think!